The Big Short:
Read the Book/
Watch the Film

John F. Sase, Ph.D.

DEDICATION

For Julie

CONTENTS

JOHN F. SASE

ACKNOWLEDGMENTS

Michael Lewis, author of *The Big Short: Inside the Doomsday Machine* (W.W. Norton. 2011) and Adam McKay, screen adaptor and director of *The Big Short* (Paramount Pictures. 2015) who have provided us with excellent educational aids for students of Money, Banking, and Financial Markets,

INTRODUCTION

Michael Lewis has written many books about real people and real events in the financial markets. In The Big Short: Inside the Doomsday Machine (W.W. Norton. 2011), Lewis does a commendable job of explaining exactly what happened in these markets between 2004 and 2008—events that drove old, established companies such as Bear Stearns and Lehman Brothers out of business while millions of Americans lost their homes in the largest mortgage meltdown in history. The Big Short reached #1 on the New York Times Bestseller List.

In 2015, Paramount Pictures released The Big Short, the film adaptation directed by Adam McKay. The movie tells a story of idiocy and greed in modern-day finance as a compelling drama with a stellar cast that includes Christian Bale, Steve Carrell, Brad Pitt, and others. McKay relates this complex story in a fast-paced and even humorous manner that lets the narrator (Greg Lippmann, played by Ryan Gosling) break the fourth wall and bring the audience along for a wild ride.

In 2016, the film won the Academy Award for Best Writing in an Adapted Screenplay (McKay and Charles Randolph). In addition, The Big Short was nominated for Best Picture, Best Actor in a Supporting Role (Christian Bale), Best Achievement in Directing (McKay), and Best Achievement in Film Editing (Hank Corwin).

As a lecturer on Money, Banking, and Financial Markets at Wayne State University and as a former Outside Director (public watchdog) of $3.5 billion of index funds at Comerica Bank throughout the 1990s, I (Dr. Sase) thought that I would put together a concordance of the book and film.

As I formed this concordance from the book, the shooting script, and the final cut of the film, something clicked inside as I discovered a fresh, viable way to explain complicated matters and events in Economics, Finance, and Law to a wide audience. In this treatment of the story, I offer you an escorted walk through the ten chapters of the book and the 130 minutes of screen time.

I want you to kick back and enjoy a splendid book and film production that incorporate the major themes of greed, stupidity, and human emotion that have been a mainstay of storytelling since the days that we sat around a fire for mutual protection against saber-tooth tigers, wooly mammoths, and other beasties.

CASE BRIEF

[SCENES 1 – 5]

While the dust from the Bubble-Burst was settling in 2008, Michael Lewis met with Meredith Whitney, an analyst on Wall Street who had predicted the collapse of Citigroup based on discussions with several of the individuals who are represented in the book and the film. Whitney also introduced Lewis to half a dozen other core insiders who had foreseen the mortgage-backed maelstrom of 2007 and 2008, who acted contrary to the prevailing market mythology that allowed this disaster to occur, and who saved the skins of themselves and many of the investors around them.

Both the book and the film narrate three separate though parallel stories about the Housing Mortgage Crisis in the United States from 2005 through 2008. Both works focus on Dr. Michael Burry, a California physician suffering from Asperger's Syndrome and Bipolar Disorder who became fascinated with the bond market coupled to mortgage-making with falling lending standards in 2004. He made the move from medicine to mortgage funds with the help of a sizeable inheritance.

Dr. Burry left his residency to create Scion Capital Hedge Fund as Fund Manager. Burry believed that the housing market was built on a bubble that would burst within a few years. Under his own autonomy, Burry proceeded to bet against the housing market. He made the rounds of major banks to develop Credit Default Swaps.

Greg Lippmann (renamed Jared Vennett for the film), an investor with Deutsche Bank, learned about what Burry was doing. Lippmann/Vennet believed that he could succeed by implementing Burry's approach. By accident, a telephone inquiry from Lipmann placed this information into the hands of Steve Eisman (renamed Mark Baum) a Corporate Attorney turned Equity Analyst turned Money Manager. [Scene 5, 00:27:40]

Eisman/Baum became one of the few to combine a knowledge of real estate and Wall Street to short (bet against) the disastrous subprime mortgage bonds of the past decade. A quasi-independent manager under the Morgan Stanley umbrella of companies, he sallied forth in order to verify the assertions made by Burry and others.

PROLOGUE

POLTERGEIST

[SCENE 1]

While working as an analyst for Oppenheimer and Company, Meredith Whitney predicted that Citigroup would fail due to gross mismanagement. On 31 October 2007, she issued a research report noting that dividends paid out to investors by the bank were greater than its profits. Whitney projected that this financial condition would lead to the bankruptcy of the firm.

Following the Mortgage Crisis of 2008, she argued that the catastrophe was caused by the inability of bankers on Wall Street to manage and allocate capital. Subsequently, Whitney shared her research and contact list with Michael Lewis.

PART ONE

CH. 1 -- A SECRET ORIGIN STORY

[SCENES 1 – 5]

Lewie Ranieri, a former bond-trader who became Vice-President of the investment firm Salomon Brothers, is considered the father of Mortgage-Backed Securities. In the Dark Ages of the 1990s, Ranieri grew a new kind of bond market by packing home mortgages into bonds known as Real-Estate Mortgage-Backed Securities (REMBS).

In addition to primary mortgages, they stimulated a market for secondary (junior) liens. These liens took the forms of equity loans and lines of credit that encouraged homeowners to tap into the unused equity of their homes. In turn, this action drove competing mortgage-interest rates to such a low level that even borrowers with marginal credit scores could obtain mortgages.

This led to a surge in the issuance of these subprime mortgages, which then were packaged into bonds that did not enjoy the assurances from the Federal Government that had been received by high-quality Mortgage-Backed Securities in past years. However, the investment market was hungry for more of these securities, which were stuffed with subprime mortgages.

Steve Eisman (Mark Baum) and his team begin to decipher the suspicious accounting that was used by the originators of the subprime mortgages and bonds. They discovered that companies were reporting expected future values as current profits in their balance sheets prematurely. Concurrently, these companies failed to reveal the accurate delinquency rate for the home loans that they were making.

These loans were being packaged into bonds. The rapid turnover between time of mortgage origination and their being sold and packaged into securities resulted in a claim-limited risk (similar to buying a horse without checking its teeth). In simpler terms, banks and mortgage companies were originating loans with highly probable default rates. These subprime mortgages then were sold to re-packagers.

However, the banks and mortgage companies left these mortgages on their books as profit. These subprime lenders were denied capital when it became scarce during the time that Russia began defaulting on its debts. Within a year, these lenders went bankrupt.

Here is a bit of background. After the Internet/High-Tech Bubble of 1999/2000, Eisman/Baum started his own hedge fund with support from Morgan Stanley. Upon finding a $50 million client, he attracted additional team members from his former firm as well as from Oppenheimer and Company.

The subprime-mortgage industry reemerged by 2005. Initially, brokers sold mortgages that had the traditional fixed rate of interest. However, mortgages with low, fixed "teaser" rates that switched to a floating rate after a few years became *en vogue*.

When the variable rate kicked in, many homebuyers found that their monthly payment doubled or even tripled. As rates changed, the total mortgage debt varied for each individual homebuyer. The mortgage market sold these new creatures (Adjustable-Rate Mortgages) to the fixed-income departments of investment banks such as Bear Stearns. In turn, these banks spun the mortgages into bonds that they sold to investors.

As a result, Eisman/Baum and his team discovered that they could make large amounts of money by shorting the stocks of subprime lenders. Essentially, Eisman/Baum and company would bet against these financial instruments, which they did not own. This action resembled a person buying fire insurance on his/her neighbor's house by speculating that it was likely to catch fire and to burn down.

CH. 2 -- IN THE LAND OF THE BLIND

[Scene 6]

Let us envision a Mortgage-Backed Security as a stack of Jenga wood blocks. [Scene 6, 00:30:00] The top layer (top tranche) is composed of mortgages that are the least at risk. Therefore, Moody's, Standard & Poor's, and the Fitch Group rank this tranche as the highest. Since it is the safest one, this tranche pays the lowest rate of interest. Therefore, investors are compensated by receiving their payments before the holders of the lower-rated, riskier tranches.

This sounds simple, right? Well, it's not, and here is why: During the early 2000s, mortgage-lending standards had fallen as interest-only and adjustable-rate subprime mortgages became increasingly available and popular. As

Michael Burry looked more closely at these mortgages, he found that the late-payment and default rates for this class of instrument were much higher than commonly thought throughout the financial market in the benchmark year of 2004, the year in which the "bizarrity" began.

In response, Burry developed the idea of the Credit Default Swap (CDS). In effect, these swaps were an "insurance policy" on subprime-filled mortgage bonds. Burry intentionally looked for bonds that were backed by the worst loans. Then, he convinced Deutche Bank and Goldman Sachs to create these CDSs and sell them to him. As the subprime mortgage-bond market began to fail, these banks requested to buy back the swaps from him.

PART TWO

CH. 3 -- HOW CAN A GUY WHO CAN'T SPEAK ENGLISH LIE?

[Scene 6, 00:31:14]

Greg Lippmann (Jared Vennet), a bond trader for Deutche Bank who claimed that he had come up with the idea of shorting home-equity bond tranches, approached Eisman/Baum in February 2006. Lippmann/Vennet explained to Eisman that, if home prices stopped rising, then large numbers of U.S. homebuyers with low-equity positions would begin to default on their mortgages as they went underwater (home price drops below outstanding loan amount).

Lippmann/Vennet says that he planned to "bet" against these home loans by purchasing

CDSs on the worst of the subprime-mortgage bonds since they were the most likely to default.

On the opposite side of these bets was a unit of American International Group (AIG). This unit had begun by selling insurance to banks as protection against the risk of default by publicly held corporations. In the first half of the 2000s, banks approached AIG with debt from credit cards and student loans.

By 2005, these loans had been eclipsed by the subprime-mortgage loans. As a result, AIG had become the largest owner of subprime-mortgage bonds. Goldman Sachs convinced AIG to service these subprime bonds by transferring all future-loss risk to AIG. In addition, Goldman Sachs created the Synthetic Subprime-Mortgage Bond-Backed Collateralized-Debt Obligation (SSMBCDO), an obtuse security that was misunderstood throughout the industry.

In each of these Obligations, Goldman Sachs gathered ground-floor tranches (the highest risk) from each of one hundred subprime stacks and positioned them into a new tower. They proceeded to convince rating agencies that all of the floors were not the same. Though separate tranches may have been dog, cat, or monkey poo, the rating agencies gave 80% of these new Obligations the best available rating.

CH. 4 -- HOW TO HARVEST A MIGRANT WORKER

[Scenes 8 – 9, Scene 9, 00:50:38]

Individuals within AIG realized that they held an overabundance of the lowest grade of bonds disguised as the highest grade. In response, AIG stopped selling CDSs on these soon-to-be-worthless Obligations.

However, the company made no effort to repair anticipated damage from those CDSs that were sold previously. AIG stopped pouring more toxic waste into a pool that was already corrosive. Nevertheless, buyers of these similar Obligations emerged in the market.

In May 2006, S&P announced that it planned to change its rating system for subprime-mortgage bonds. In response, housing prices began to fall in July of that year. However, CDS prices (insurance premiums) also fell, contrary to financial logic. Eisman/Baum and his team searched for the worst of the worst subprime-mortgage bonds so that they could purchase the best CDSs (insurance policies) on them.

They discovered that the pools containing the largest number of fraudulent loans, those lacking documentation, received floating interest rates. These pools were concentrated in Arizona, California, Florida, and Nevada. [Scene 8, 00:43:20]

Burry, Eisman/Baum, and Lippman/Vennet alleged that certain firms on Wall Street wanted these high-risk, low-grade mortgages (graded triple-B by Moody's S&P, and Fitch) in order to package them with low-risk, high-grade (graded triple-A) mortgages.

The intent was to receive a high-grade, triple-A rating for the entire pool. To investigate their personal allegation, Eisman/Baum and his team met with Moody's and S&P. In the film, members of the team visit with an unnamed woman at Moody's (portrayed as S&P in the film) who is responsible for the ratings on many of these CDOs. This woman tells her visitors that she is not allowed to downgrade any of the ratings without permission from her superiors. [Scene 11, 01:04:14]

PART THREE

CH. 5 -- ACCIDENTAL CAPITALISTS

[Scenes 7 & 10]

In 2003, Charlie Ledley (Geller) and Jamie Mai (Shipley) started their Cornwall Capital Management (Brownfield) with $110,000 and built it up into a bit more serious money. [Scene 10, 00:57:02] However, the duo had difficulties doing larger trades because they did not have the capital needed to trade with firms on Wall Street. [Scene 7, 00:37:37]

Mentor, neighbor, and soon-to-be partner Ben Hockett (Rickert) had inside experience on Wall Street. [Scene 7, 00:41:50] He persuaded Deutche Bank to put Cornwall on their institutional-trading platform.

The small firm began by betting against the upper tranches of CDOs. Though Ledley and Mai may have lacked sophisticated insight, their own instincts and the analytical support from Hockett brought them to realize that an implosion in the market was imminent.

Huge profits were to be made by betting against (purchasing CDSs) the upper tranches of CDOs that had weak underbellies. By January 2007, Cornwall Capital owned $110 million in CDSs on the top tranche of asset-backed CDOs.

CH. 6 -- SPIDERMAN AT THE VENETIAN

[SCENES 12 – 14]

In Las Vegas, Eisman/Baum and company attended a conference for bond-market brokers and a dinner hosted by Deutche Bank and Lippman/Vennet. [Scene 12, 01:12:08] There, Eisman/Baum learned that CDO managers represented the interests of the traders on Wall Street who funded them and who supplied them with the CDOs.

In addition, he discovered that these CDO managers did not take risks themselves and did not represent the interests of their clients. [Scene 14, 01:22:54] From this epiphany, Eisman/Baum finally understood the other side of Credit Default Swaps.

A CDS was used as a "replicate" of a Mortgage-Backed Security (MBS). Wall Street was using the income from selling Collateralized Debt Swaps to synthesize more bonds that in turn would need to be insured. [Scene 14, 01:26:03]

Here is a simpler explanation: MBS --> CDO --> CDS --> Synthesized Collateralized Debt Obligation. Furthermore, Eisman/Baum and company discovered that the goal of the rating agencies was to maximize the number of investment instruments that they rated—in other words, the more that they rated, the more that they got paid.

In addition to maximizing the fees received for rating, the agencies sought to maximize income from tracking these same bonds after their Initial Public Offering (IPO). Was this a slight conflict of interest?

PART FOUR

CH. 7 -- THE GREAT TREASURE HUNT

[SCENES 16 – 17]

In January 2006, CDS IndexCo and Markit—companies that provide asset information, indices, pricing, and reference-data--launched ABX.HE, a subprime mortgage-backed credit-derivative index that focused on home-equity loans as assets. [Scene 5, 00:28:20]

A year later, subprime-mortgage bonds had lost more than 30% of their value. The ABX fell by more than a point on 31 January 2007. Charlie Ledley (Geller) and Jamie Mai (Shipley) assumed that the triple-B-rated CDOs would collapse as well.

Instead, firms on Wall Street went contrary to this logic. They created and sold an additional $50 billion in new CDOs. Shortly thereafter, Morgan Stanley sent a list of AA (double-A) tranches of CDOs on which the bank was willing to sell CDSs (insurance).

Basically, the banks were betting against themselves. After Ledley/Geller and Mai/Shipley figured this out with the help of Ben Hockett/Rickert, they purchased a large number of CDSs for their company, Cornwall Capital.

An additional trade with Wachovia Bank for $45 million left Cornwall with $205 million in CDSs by late February 2007. In March of 2006, Cornwall Capital had bet that Bear Stearns would collapse by purchasing $105 million in CDSs on Bear Stearns from the Hong Kong and Shanghai Banking Corporation Limited (HSBC). On 14 June 2007, Bear Stearns decided to sell $3.8 billion of subprime-mortgage CDSs and then close their fund, which was losing money.

Having started out with a $60 million equity fund, Eisman/Baum had shorted $600 million and wanted to short more. He learned that the rating agencies actually were rating bonds backed by Adjustable-Rate Mortgages (ARMs) higher than similar bonds that were backed by fixed-rate mortgages.

Furthermore, Eisman/Baum discovered that the rating agencies assumed that home prices would continue to rise. However, Eisman/Baum and company watched their positions move by millions of dollars per day as the Subprime-MBS market declined again in June.

On 17 June 2007, investors in the hedge fund owned by Bear Stearns were told that their Subprime AAA-rated CDOs were worthless. Eisman/Baum smiled.

CH. 8 -- THE LONG QUIET

[Scene 16]

In 2007, subprime loans were defaulting in vast numbers because the teaser rates from 2005 were switching to adjustable rates. Investors were calling Michael Burry to ask for their money back. They wanted out of his short funds.

Dr. Burry sent his list of CDSs (the swaps) to the large banks for the purpose of showing this list to potential buyers through 2006. He did this in order to get an idea of the current market price for his CDS.

Contrary to financial logic, he found that the price of insuring the loans underlying the bonds still was falling, though the loans underlying the bonds were going bad at a fast pace. Burry finally realized what Eisman/Baum had come to discover independently.

The banks themselves were on the other side of the CDS (swap) bets, using the proceeds from the CDSs to create more and more CDOs (subprime-mortgage bonds) of dubious quality.

Almost half of the $555 million that Burry managed could be withdrawn by his investors in the fourth quarter of 2006 or the first two quarters of 2007. Though his investors wanted to withdraw their money, the agreement between these investors and Burry gave him the right to keep their money if it was invested in securities that were not tradeable freely.

During the spring, the profit of Burry's Scion Capital was up 18% as teaser rates reset on subprime mortgages. [Scene 16, 01:36:10]

As we have seen, hedge funds failed at Bear Stearns on 14 June 2007. In their wake, the index for publicly traded BBB-rated bonds fell by more than 19%.

Morgan Stanley contacted Burry, asking to purchase whatever CDSs that he held at Scion. Meanwhile, Burry discovered that Goldman

Sachs had reversed their position from betting on subprime mortgages to betting against them.

The Big Short was afoot! One-third of subprime-mortgage borrowers defaulted on their loans by December 2007. This final event wiped out the bonds that Burry, Eisman/Baum, and others had bet against. They smiled.

PART FIVE

Ch. 9 -- A DEATH OF INTEREST

[Scenes 16 – 19]

In 2004, Morgan Stanley had created subprime-mortgage bonds, CDOs, at a faster rate than they could acquire mortgages to fill them. This shortage of input often created a delay between the buying of mortgage loans and the selling of mortgage-backed CDOs.

In turn, this led to a price-change risk in a fluctuating market. In order to avoid potential profit losses resulting from this time gap, Morgan created CDOs composed the BBB-rated loans and then sold CDSs (insurance) for these CDOs to clients at a profit of 2.5% per annum.

The contracts on these swaps were most curious. These contracts were written in such a way that indicated that Morgan was not making a bet on the entire pool of the underlying bonds. Rather, the bank shorted (bet against) only the last outstanding mortgage-loan in the pool.

In the given market at that time, it is possible that Morgan did not understand that these CDOs would fail to produce a payoff.

Bond-trader Howie Hubler (not represented in the film) managed the asset-backed trading at Morgan Stanley. Given his superior track record, Morgan offered Hubler a profit-sharing deal in which he would create Global Proprietary Credit Group (GPCG) within Morgan Stanley in order to manage the subprime-mortgage CDOs in 2006.

In the following year, Hubler came to realize that the premiums on the CDSs (similar to an insurance-policy premium) that Morgan paid to the owners of BBB-rated CDOs diminished the profits of GPCG. Therefore, Hubler sold off these CDOs in favor of AAA-rated CDOs that required the payment of lower premiums.

(Note: These triple-A CDOs were comprised mostly of high-risk triple-B mortgage loans).

One of the largest subprime lenders, New Century, declared bankruptcy in April 2007. [Scene 16, 01:35:09] Subsequently, Hubler sold more than one-third of the $16 billion AAA-rated CDOs held by GPCG to Bear Stearns.

A month later, Hubler and his team projected a potential loss of $2.7 billion if the underlying subprime-mortgage loans were to default by a greater magnitude than expected. In July 2007, Morgan Stanley learned that it owed $1.2 billion to Deutsche Bank on a $4 billion CDO trade that was made earlier by Hubler.

Based on its response to Deutche Bank, Morgan appears not to have understood the deal because they refused to settle the matter with Deutsche. Shortly thereafter, underlying subprime-mortgage loans began to default by a great magnitude. This caused the supported CDOs to fail in vast numbers. As the dust cleared, Morgan Stanley had lost $9 billion on the $16 billion of CDOs that had been traded by Hubler.

In addition to these woes, shareholders sued Bear Stearns in connection to the collapse of its subprime-backed hedge funds. The small firm of Cornwall Capital owned CDSs (insurance policies) on almost two dozen CDOs.

However, Cornwall would suffer great losses if the market were to rebound. Hockett/Rickert searched for buyers of CDSs that Cornwall had bought for $1 million. Calling UBS and other firms on Wall Street, Hockett offered to sell these CDSs to them. [Scene 18, 01:46:19]

These firms appeared desperate to obtain insurance on the failing subprime-mortgage bonds that they held. The firms purchased the CDSs and assumed the risk that Bear Stearns might fail. Suddenly, the CDSs that Cornwall Capital had purchased for $1 million were worth $60 million.

Dr. Burry sold his CDOs as well and he would realize profits of $720 million by the end of 2007. The market continued to unravel through June of 2008. During that summer, the International Monetary Fund determined that the losses on U.S. subprime-related assets totaled $1 trillion.

CH. 10 -- TWO MEN IN A BOAT

[SCENES 19 – 20]

By December 2007, Eisman/Baum and company had doubled the size of its short fund to $1.5 billion. [Scene 19, 01:49:37] On 14 March 2008, Bear Stearns collapsed. Then, Lehman Brothers declared bankruptcy on 18 September.

Major losses on that Margin-Call date included: $50 billion for Merrill Lynch, $60 billion for Citigroup, and $9 billion for Morgan Stanley. By the beginning of the New Year, Bank of America had completed its acquisition of Merrill Lynch.

In response to a deep decline in the U.S. stock market during mid-to-late September

2008, the Federal Reserve Board announced that it had given $85 billion to AIG in order to pay off its losses on the CDSs (the swaps) that it had sold. [Scene 20, 01:58:56]

Meanwhile, the stocks of Goldman Sachs and Morgan Stanley plummeted by 10% to 17%. Those parties that bet against the subprime-mortgage bonds fared much better. Cornwall Capital had quadrupled its holdings to $135 million. Dr. Burry earned $750 million for his investors on the $600 million that he managed.

By the beginning of October 2008, the U.S. government announced that it would not allow any of the large firms on Wall Street to fail. They didn't. [Scene 20, 02:00:18] On 3 October, the Feds invoked the Troubled Asset Relief Program (TARP). This initiative gave purchasing power of $700 billion to the U.S. Treasury to buy illiquid mortgage-backed securities and other assets. This was done in order to restore liquidity in the money markets.

EPILOGUE

Salomon Brothers was an investment bank that was founded on Wall Street in 1910. In the 1980s, then-managing partner John Gutfreund took it from a private partnership to a publicly traded corporation.

During this restructuring process, the Salomon Brothers partnership was acquired by the Phibro Corporation, a commodity-trading firm. This combination morphed into a new entity that was renamed Salomon Inc., with Gutfreund as its first CEO.

Gutfreund's initiative had started a trend on Wall Street that resulted in private investment companies going public. Michael Lewis asked Gutfreund if he thought that taking Salomon public had been the first step on a path that led to financial catastrophe. Gutfreund agreed, stating that he had helped to create a monster by transferring the risk from the partners of Salomon to the shareholders of Salomon Inc.

TAKEAWAY

An important lesson that we can learn from the book and film of The Big Short is that not all financial disasters have their roots in the conspiracy of a few masterminds. Sometimes, an economic unraveling is the result of simple-minded greed and stupidity in an imperfect system that has evaded pragmatic and necessary regulation for the benefit of the wider community.

Sometimes the smoking gun is nothing more than a limp pickle. Let's put it this way: Structure of a firm begets Conduct and Conduct begets Performance. When the underlying structure of a firm allows idiocrasy, then perhaps it is time to repair or even to rebuild the structure.

In the least, we like to think that entities such as LLCs and PLCs, which remain prevalent within Law, Economics, and other fields, ensure a higher degree of personal responsibility than the corporate form of business. Perhaps we need to solve the inhuman problems that result from a creature that gained human rights via the 14th Amendment more than a century ago.

ABOUT THE AUTHOR

After completing an undergraduate degree in Liberal Arts, Dr. Sase earned a double Masters in Business Economics and Administration, followed by a Ph.D. in Economics with concentrations in Urban and Industrial Organization Economics. Over the decades, He has taught more than ten thousand students and has taken an active role in a number of for-profit and non-profit organizations. Since 1997, Dr. Sase has helped attorneys by providing determination in 500 cases, has given a hundred depositions, and has testified a couple dozen times in both state and federal courts.